Copyright © 2015 by **Gabi Rupp**

DISCLAIMER: This book contains material protected under International and Federal Copyright Laws and Treaties. Any unauthorized reprint or use of this material is prohibited. No part of this book may be reproduced or transmitted in any form or by any means, electronic or mechanical, including photocopying, recording, or by any information storage and retrieval system without express written permission from the publisher.

Dear reader,
this is a book to always carry with you
and cherish, to be there whenever you need
to be uplifted. Enjoy insightful, inspirational,
and famous quotes to restore your hope.
These carefully selected quotations will
give you hope, comfort and build your faith.

Thank you and feel the power of enduring hope!

Gabi Rupp

Prayer is a bridge
from despair to hope.
~Bill Hybels

Be joyful in hope,
patient in affliction,
faithful in prayer.
~Romans 12:12

Faith, hope and love
are the roots of the tree of life
- of our spiritual life.
~Mother Julia

"Hope is good. Without it, well, you do
the math. But hope has to be like a prayer.
Putting it out there to something
more powerful than yourself."
~Lisa Unger

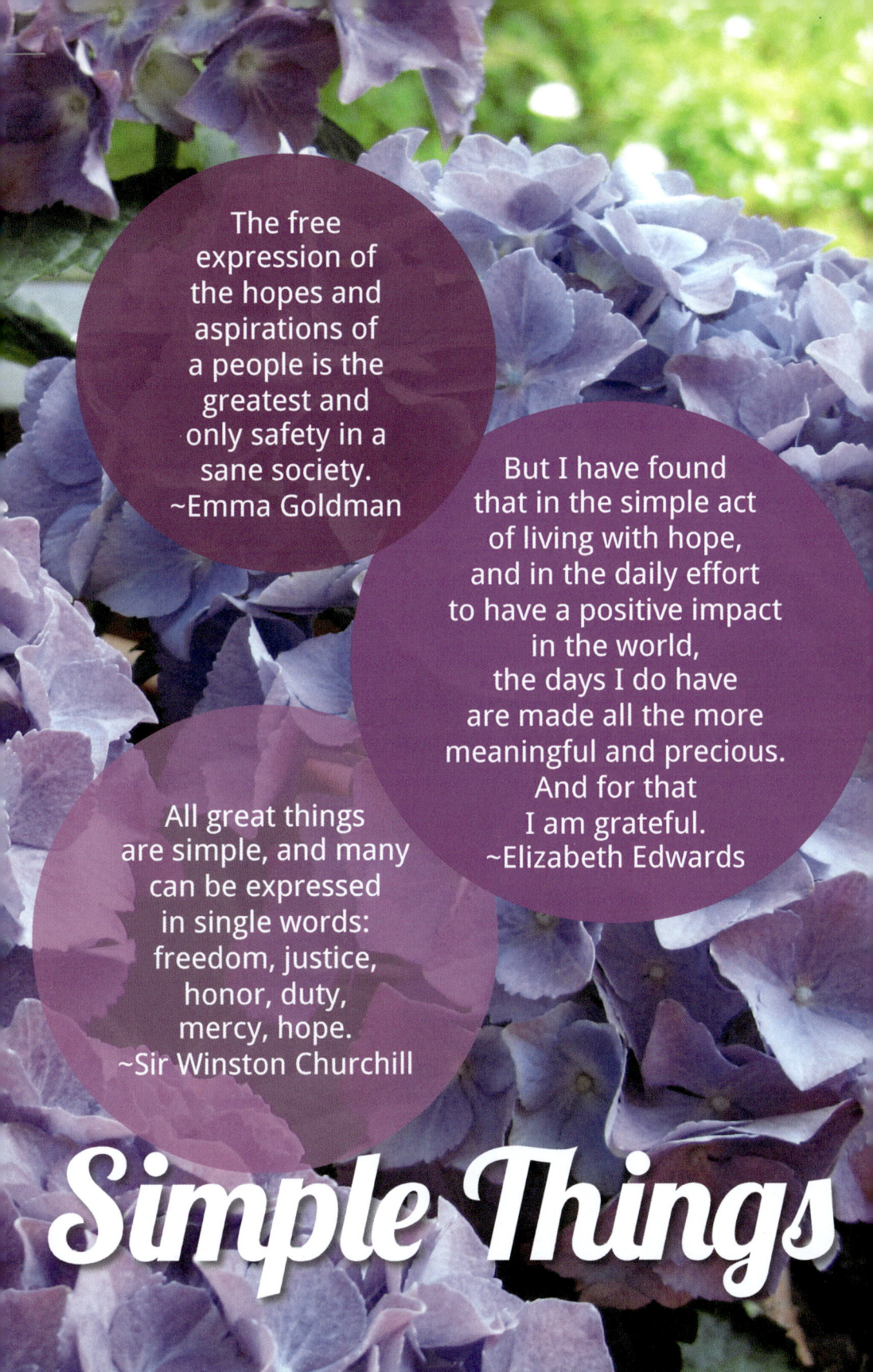

So many tangles in life are ultimately hopeless that we have no appropriate sword other than laughter.
~Gordon William Allport

Hope lies in dreams,
in imagination,
and in the courage
of those who dare
to make dreams
into reality.
~Jonas Salk

Hope is the thing with feathers –
that perches in the soul –
and sings the tune without words –
and never stops, at all.
~Emily Elizabeth Dickinson

Hope is the pillar
that holds up the world.
Hope is the dream
of a waking man.
~Pliny

Hope is the
poor man's bread.
~George Herbert

The miserable have
no other medicine
but only hope.
~Friedrich W. Nietzsche

The question was
put to him, what hope is
and his answer was,
The dream
of a waking man.
~Laertius Diogenes

Dream

Hope itself is a species of happiness,
and perhaps, the chief happiness
which this world affords.
~Samuel Johnson

They say a person
needs just three things
to be truly happy in this world:
someone to love,
something to do, and
something to hope for.
~Tom Bodett

At the end of our time on earth,
if we have lived fully,
we will not be able to say,
"I was always happy".
Hopefully we will be able to say,
"I have experienced a lifetime of real moments,
and many of them were happy moments."
~Barbara DeAngelis

Children

All kids need is a little help, a little hope and somebody who believes in them
~Earvin Johnson

Young people have an almost biological destiny to be hopeful.
~Marshall Ganz

The central struggle of parenthood is to let our hopes for our children outweigh our fears.
~Ellen Goodman

Purpose

What oxygen is to the lungs, such is hope to the meaning of life.
~Emil Brunner

Hope is not the conviction that something will turn out well, but the certainty that something makes sense, regardless of how it turns out.
~Václav Havel

Without God, life has no purpose, and without purpose, life has no meaning. Without meaning, life has no significance or hope.
~Rick Warren

Hope is both the earliest and the most indispensable virtue inherent in the state of being alive. If life is to be sustained hope must remain, even where confidence is wounded, trust impaired.
~Erik H. Erikson

Don't give up!

Nothing is hopeless, we must hope for everything.
~Madeleine L'Engle

Never deprive someone of hope; it might be all they have.
~H. Jackson Brown Jr.

Hope is necessary in every condition.
~Samuel Johnson

Everything that is done in the world is done by hope.
~Martin Luther

Most of the important things in the world have been accomplished by people who have kept on trying when there seemed to be no hope at all.
~Dale Carnegie

Influence

A leader is a dealer in hope.
~Napoleon Bonaparte

A good storyteller is a person who has a good memory and hopes other people haven't.
~Irvin S. Cobb

The influence of a beautiful, helpful, hopeful character is contagious and may revolutionize a whole town.
~Eleanor H. Porter

Each time someone stands up for an ideal, or acts to improve the lot of others, or strikes out against injustice, he sends forth a tiny ripple of hope.
~Robert F. Kennedy

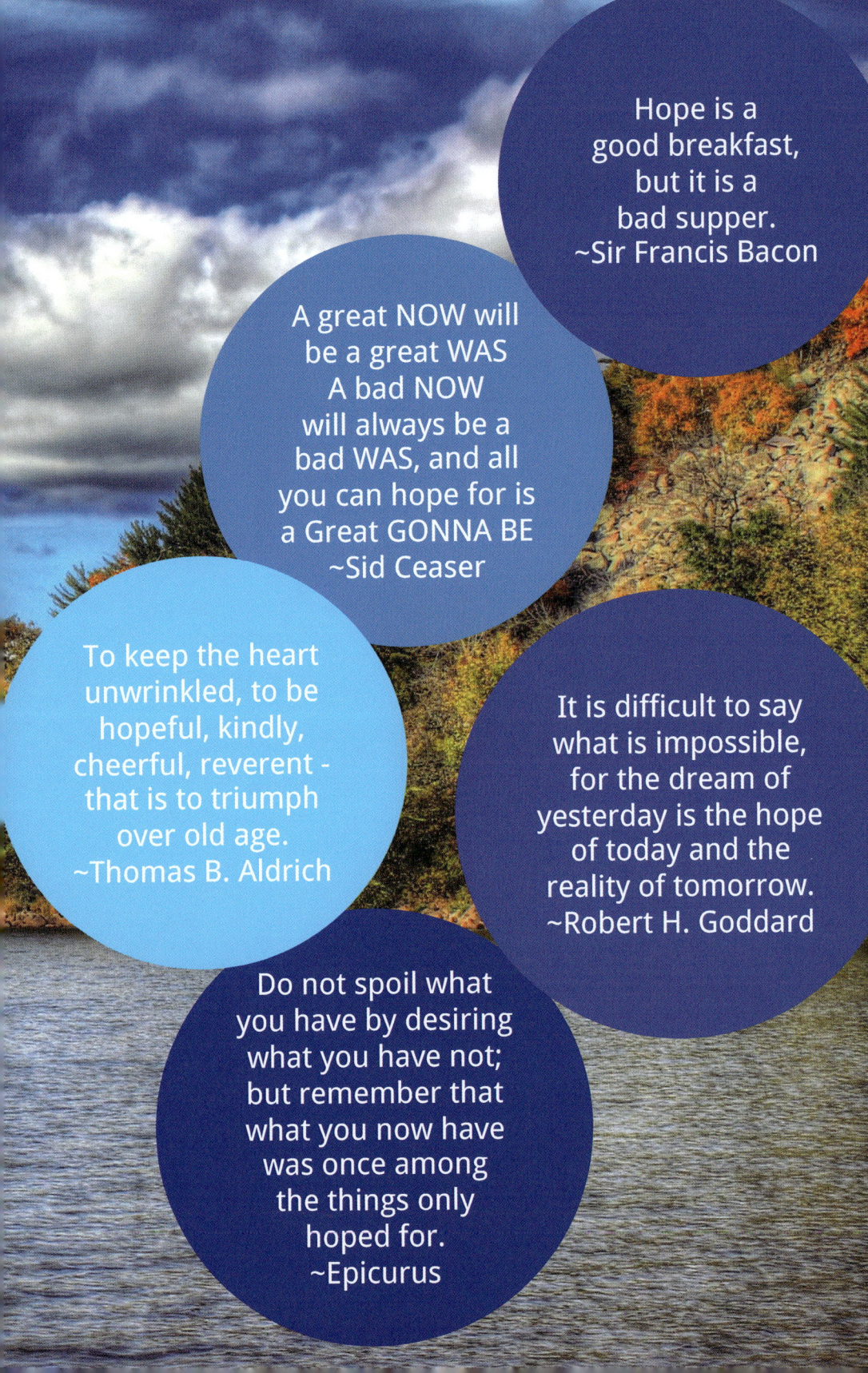

He has no hope
who never had a fear.
~William Cowper

Fear less, hope more;
Whine less, breathe more;
Talk less, say more;
Hate less, love more;
And all good things are yours.
~Swedish Proverb

We promise according to our hopes
and perform according to our fears.
~Author Unknown

Hope and fear are inseparable.
There is no hope without fear,
nor any fear without hope.
~La Rochefoucauld

Hope is nature's veil for hiding truth's nakedness.
~Alfred B. Nobel

Hope provides comfort, and hope does not always require probability.
~John Perry

Hope is the only universal liar who never loses his reputation for veracity.
~Robert Green Ingersoll

Comfort

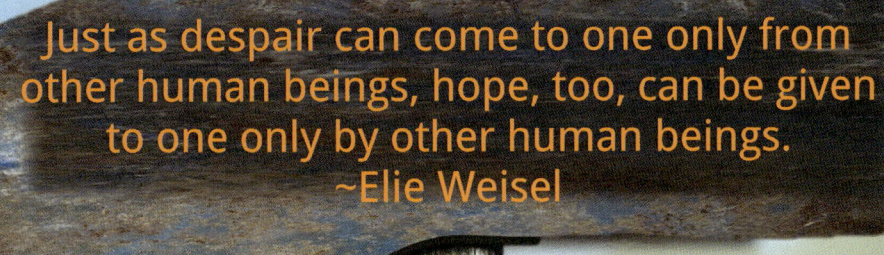

Just as despair can come to one only from other human beings, hope, too, can be given to one only by other human beings.
~Elie Weisel

Appetite, with an opinion of attaining, is called hope; the same, without such opinion, despair.
~Thomas Hobbes

We must accept finite disappointment, but never lose infinite hope.
~Martin Luther King Jr.

Despair

He who does not hope
to win has already lost.
~Jose Joaquin de Olmedo

Whoever does not love
his work cannot hope
that it will please others.
~Unknown

Hope is the companion of power,
and mother of success;
for who so hopes strongly
has within him the gift of miracles.
~Samuel Smiles

If you wish to succeed in life,
make perseverance your bosom friend,
experience your wise counselor,
caution your elder brother,
and hope your guardian genius.
~Joseph Addison

Success

HOPE
IS ONLY THE
love of life

HENRI-FREDERIC AMIEL

Men and women are limited not by the place of their birth, not by the color of their skin, but by the size of their hope.
~John Johnson

Let us hope that we are all preceded in this world by a love story.
~Don Snyder

If it were not for hope, the heart would break.
~Thomas Fuller

Love lives on hope, and dies when hope is dead.
~Pierre Corneille

But groundless hope, like unconditional love, is the only kind worth having.
~John P. Barlow

Wisdom

Hope for miracles,
but don't rely on one.
~Yiddish Proverb

There are no hopeless situations;
There are only people who have
grown hopeless about them.
~Clare Boothe Luce

The sum of all human wisdom is contained
in these two words: Wait and Hope.
~Alexander Dumas

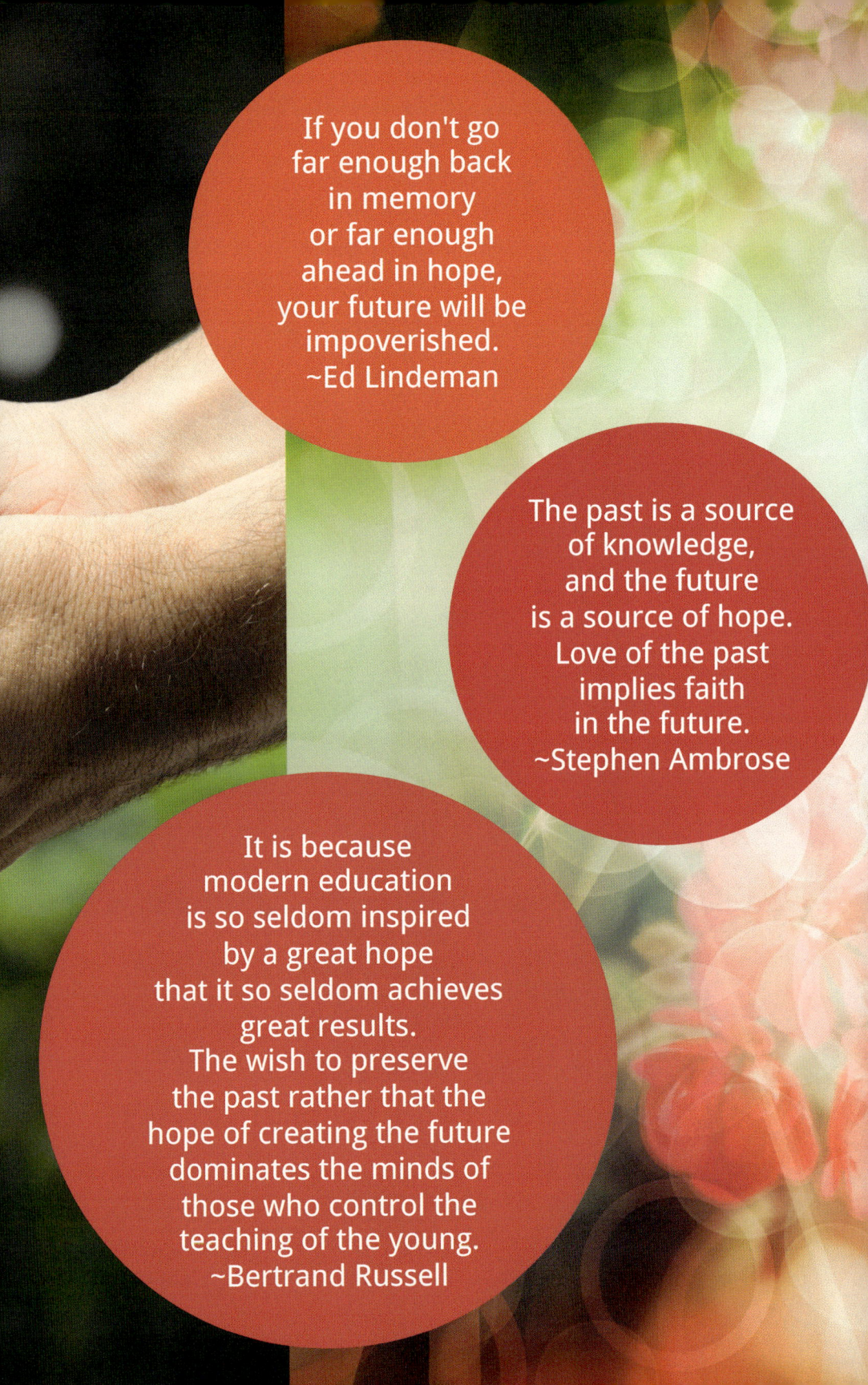

SUBSCRIBE TO MY NEWSLETTER!

Hello! What's your name? It's nice to meet you!
I'd love to send you each week
new inspirational quotes, easy healthy recipes
and also advanced tips to make healthy habits stick.
I'm very much looking forward to seeing
you there again. Until then I'm wishing you
all the best and enjoy!

SIGN UP TODAY

http://leanjumpstart.com/newsletter

OTHER TITLES YOU MIGHT LIKE:

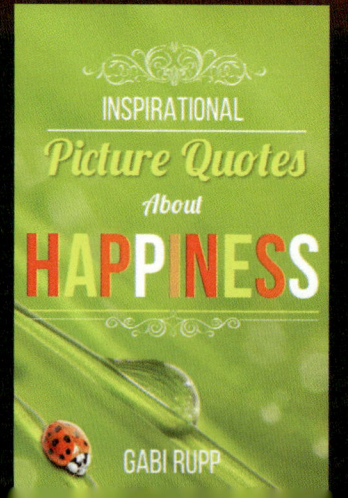
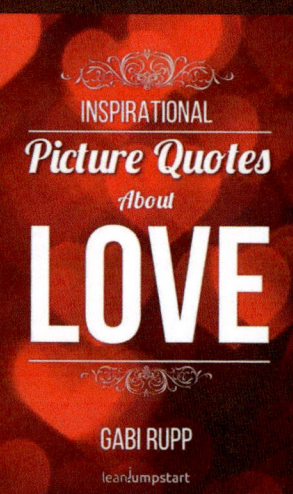
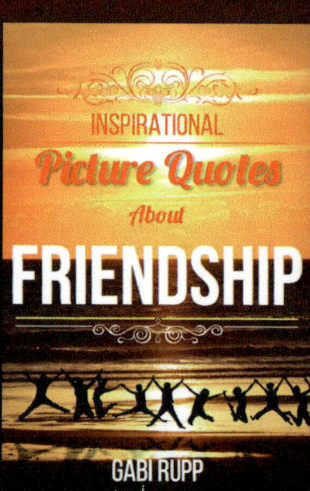

Gabi Rupp is a certified coach, author and entrepreneur. Prior to her work online, Gabi spent more than a decade as a marketing executive, mostly in the food and nutrition field, helping her clients realize their own projects. After her daughter was born, she found her true calling: writing, teaching, and coaching. Having the perfect life/work balance gave her the freedom to be a fulltime mother. In 2013 she founded www.leanjumpstart.com, where she uses a successful combination of proven science and practical experience to help people get in shape and stick with their new, healthy habits. Gabi is now happily settled in a little German town near the beautiful Black Forest region and spends her days with family, friends, and assisting clients as they overcome limitations and live life to its fullest potential.

Publisher: Gabi Rupp, Leanjumpstart.com / gabi@leanjumpstart.com
Concept, Design & Layout: Gabi Rupp
Photo Credits: Footage Firm Inc., Dollar Photo Club ©: arinahabich, Ocskay Bence, diego cervo, Frantab, karelnoppe, Gabi Rupp, sibadanpics, Romolo Tavani, viperagp, Lisa F. Young
1. Edition 2015

ISBN-13: 978-1511970594
ISBN-10: 1511970596
© Gabi Rupp

Printed in Great Britain
by Amazon.co.uk, Ltd.,
Marston Gate.